THE VERY NEXT THING

FOLLOW GOD. WHERE YOU ARE. RIGHT NOW.

SIX-WEEK DEVOTIONAL

MARK HALL

PASTOR AND LEAD SINGER OF

CASTING CROWNS

with TIM LUKE

✝ **LIFESONG** ®
PUBLISHING

CONTENTS

A Simple Reminder

Not long ago, one of my Twitter posts summed up my frustration with the body of Christ today:

> **Sometimes I wish the book of Acts would be called the Book of Works so we would get up off of our grace and do something.**

Don't worry—I believe Ephesians 2:8-9. I believe it is by grace through faith that we are saved. But I think that, too often, we stop there and don't continue on to the very next verse, which says that we were created by God and then saved by grace *in order to do good works*. We also forget James 2, which says that faith without works is dead. Being a follower of Christ means accepting the free gift of grace he offers. But, as my tweet reminded, being a follower of Christ means we actually follow him into whatever he's doing.

One of the lessons I learned from reading Henry Blackaby's *Experiencing God* when I was a young man is that God is always at work. "My Father is working until now, and I am working," Jesus said in John 5:17. This revelation resonated with me because I had always been long on plans and short on follow-through.

I can't tell you how many times I answered a moment of spiritual inspiration with a personal pep talk.

"All right, this is it. I'm giving all of this to God. I'm going to let go and let him have all of me. I know what he says is true. I know I can trust him. I know what all the songs say and all these verses say. I believe it in my heart. It's time to go. Like right now. I mean it's on. For real this time. Let's do this.

"OK, maybe next week."

We believers hear loud and clear the message of knowing God and making him known. We correctly believe our position in Christ is secure for eternity. We make huge proclamations like,

I want to be all in for Jesus.
I want to be on fire for God.
I want to give him everything.
I want to lay my life at his feet.

All of us have said or felt such giant statements.

Yet there's a disconnect between what we say in moments of spiritual fervor and how we live day-to-day. If we're being honest, we follow those big statements with a few authentic questions.

What do I do next?
What comes after I say "Amen" to prayers?

How do I give God my all?

Exactly how do I lay my life at his feet?

The simple answer to those questions, if followed consistently and humbly, will change your life. If practiced by every believer, it will start a revolution. The way to follow Jesus, to lay down your life, to be on fire for God, to let him have all of you—the way to surrender all and fulfill the enormous cries of your heart is to do one thing.

The very next thing.

This is not some new revelation from God. It's a simple reminder, in a simple book, to remember to listen for God's still small voice and then do what he says. Just do the very next thing you sense he's telling you to do. You already know exactly the kinds of moments to which I'm referring because you've felt the tug in your heart before.

See that girl over there? Go ask her how she's doing. Tell her about me.

See that man? Ask him how you can pray for him.

You know that neighbor you never have time for? Invite her to supper. Build a relationship.

The coworker you had that tiff with? Go apologize. Show her who I am.

Remember when your annoying relative mentioned he wasn't sure how he was going to pay his power bill this month? He was asking for help. Pick up the phone.

It's a mistake to think that God is preparing us for some great task in the future. God always prepares us, but that preparation is not just God's process. It's his end. He is molding us into the image of Jesus over the course of our day-in-day-out lives.

You may indeed go on the mission field one day, but you need to understand that the mission field isn't somewhere else. The mission field is where your feet are at this moment. He's put you right where you are for a reason. He doesn't expect you to prepare for what you're going to do "someday" for Jesus. He expects you to listen for the very next thing that he's asking you to do, and do that.

This small book aims to help. For the next six weeks, you'll find encouragement and inspiration to take simple steps of faith in your walk with the Lord. Each week begins with a Sunday Prelude to set the stage for short daily devotionals. The week's key passages are listed after the Sunday Prelude in case you want a head start on the Scripture reading.

Each day, I encourage you to read the designated Scripture passage first. Then read the daily devotional and meditate on the Scripture and the devotional. After each devotional, space is provided for you to jot down your thoughts to the following prompts:

✝ Where do I see myself in this?
✝ What is the next step God is showing me?
✝ My prayer…

I've been a youth pastor for more than 25 years. My song-writing always has been tied to truths I feel led to teach my students and other believers, so the encouragement in this book is connected to the messages in my songs on the latest Casting Crowns album, *The Very Next Thing*.

We're all in different stages of "next" in our walks with Jesus. Regardless of where you are in your journey, this book will encourage you in your progress. I believe that the most basic step toward fulfilling the deepest desires of your heart is to maintain daily devotional time with the Lord. I call it my Quiet Time. If you don't already have a daily Quiet Time, I believe that's the very next thing that God is asking you to do first. This book can help you develop that practice.

If you are in Christ, you are a child of God. That is who you are. But that also means you must follow Christ. That is what you do. All at once, following him can be the most frightening, difficult, and ridiculously easy and freeing thing you've ever done. But just know that it is a thing you *do*.

It's the very next thing.

WHAT IF I GAVE EVERYTHING?

SUNDAY PRELUDE

I RECENTLY WATCHED a video of Secretariat, the fastest racehorse that ever lived, win the 1973 Triple Crown in the Belmont Stakes. He won by 31 lengths. That means they could've fit 31 horses between Secretariat and the second-place horse. It's the only time I remember seeing the finish line camera pan back to find the rest of the field after the winner crossed. After all these years, Secretariat still holds the record time for the Kentucky Derby, the Preakness, and the Belmont Stakes—all three legs of the Triple Crown.

As inspiring as it was to watch Secretariat break the track record by an astonishing 2.6 seconds, the video didn't show what happened first.

Right before the start of any horse race, track hands coax the giant animals into tight little metal chutes that appear to be about three feet wide. Their jockeys are mounted, trying to keep the horses calm, and you can feel the tension build as the horses step in place and snap their heads up and down. They have blinders fastened around their eyes so they will look straight ahead. They fidget and fuss as the handlers close the gate behind them, and the horses bang against the metal.

In the instant the front gates open, those massive horses explode out of the chutes. It is so violent that it looks like the gates have hidden catapults. The horses are so well trained that they look sculpted. As they strain toward top speed, they look like a sheer layer of fur wrapped around the most exquisitely developed physical bodies on the planet. The thunder of their hooves and the chorus of their snorts combine to sound like a train roaring down the tracks.

And that's when I think of the Church.

When I see Secretariat, I see what the Church of Jesus Christ can look like. I see packing people into worship and small groups, reminding them why they're here, training them to do what they're designed to do, getting them excited about God's will, and unleashing them on the world.

We should never tire of hearing and believing that our past is forgiven.

I don't want that to sound jaded or tired. I know you've heard descriptions of how the Church "should" look countless times before, and that's part of our struggle. We should never tire of hearing and believing that our past is forgiven, that God has made us a new creation, and that he can work in our weaknesses. We should never stop believing that we are God's saints in this world, his change agents, his pride and joy. We should never gloss over the beauty and power of the finest developed body on the planet—the body of Christ.

But we act as if we do tire of it. We act as if we have drowned in our clichés, that we really don't know what to do when we hear that we should get out there and…

Be on fire for God.
Give everything to him.
Lay our lives at his feet.
Do big things for God.

It's like every week we're led into our chutes in the starting gate. We enjoy stirring music and an inspiring message. We're ready to go anywhere and do anything. And then the gate opens.

But instead of bolting down a track, it's as if we're all released into a giant open field. We give it everything we've got and run as hard as we can—toward somewhere, anywhere, or nowhere in general. Where are we going? No one has any idea.

It would be like watching a gate full of thoroughbreds take off and run, only to crisscross and collide with each other. They run as fast as they can and bang into each other until they slowly realize they're not sure where they're supposed to go or what they're supposed to do. And all you have left is a big field of horses—just like every other big field of horses.

That's not God's design for us. I'm not saying that he has a specific lane for our lives and that if we get out of that lane then we're out of his will. God gives us great freedom to live and to serve him. Yet too many of us perpetually wonder to ourselves, "What if I truly abandoned myself to Jesus and threw myself onto the God who promises not to fail me? What if I stopped looking to myself, to other people, and to this world for fulfillment? What if I gave everything?"

This is the deepest heart's cry of most believers. So it's a great place to start.

Key Passages of the Week: 1 SAMUEL 17:1-54; ACTS 9:1-26

The Most Important Next Step

Teach me, O Lord, the way of your statutes; and I will keep it to the end.
Psalm 119:33

If we believers don't know what we're supposed to do next, we're like a horse with no track.

These days we're scared to death to tell people there is a step they might need to take. But there most definitely *is* a step that you need to take, and there most certainly are things you will have to *do*. The Church has been talking for decades about how saved we are, but the fruit of that has not been impressive. The Apostle Paul taught that a true understanding of grace would spur us on to follow Jesus wholeheartedly—not inspire us to sit back and enjoy our security.

I do not diminish the undeniable truths of the believer's secure position in Christ. But our secure position is a place of action, not passivity. There is a will to follow. There is a gift you've been given. There is a story you have to tell. There is a person you need to tell it to, and it's all right there in front of you.

In one of my previous books, *Thrive*, I shared that the most important next step for any believer is to cultivate a more intimate knowledge of God and his Word. We need to dig deep into Scripture and establish a pattern of consistent prayer and worship to know God and his promises and encouragement, and also to know who we are in him.

Still, knowing God and making him known consists of more than just getting saved and proclaiming, "I'm gonna do everything God says." When it comes to doing the very next thing God says, we need a Scriptural foundation or else we'll think every crazy idea that pops in our heads is from God. When our roots are in Scripture, we don't launch out on our every fantasy. Besides, our first priority every day should be to know God more.

When it comes to doing the very next thing God says, we need a Scriptural foundation.

Psalm 119:33 says, "Teach me, O Lord, the way of your statutes, and I will keep it to the end." The antecedent to the pronoun "it" is "the way." There is a way lighted by God's Word, which is why the earliest Christians were known as followers of "the Way." It's the same reason the embodiment of the Word, Jesus Christ, called himself "the way" in John 14:6.

The spiritual disciplines of Bible study, prayer, and worship are our road map to "the Way," and no shortcut exists. It takes daily discipline to deepen our fellowship with Christ. In this way, our identity—our being—is helped daily by our doing.

NEXT STEPS

✝ Where do I see myself in this?

✝ What is the next step God is showing me?

✝ My prayer:

HEBREWS 12:1-6

RUN TO FINISH

Let us also lay aside every weight, and sin which clings so closely….
HEBREWS 12:1

BEFORE THE SONG "Voice of Truth" was called by that name on Casting Crowns' first album, it existed as a simpler version called "Fear." It was the same verses with the same melody you hear now, but it portrayed an inner struggle about many of my insecurities. It was sort of a journal entry set to music, and it was not until I met Steven Curtis Chapman that it finally found some resolution.

"Man, it sounds like this is pointing you to truth," he said after listening to the lyrics. Together we came up with the chorus that brings hope to verses that depict frustration and fear. The song's message came from that dilemma we often face in a church service when we know God is moving in our hearts. We sense that nudge. We hear God's whisper. But we're afraid of what comes next.

> *Oh what I would do to have*
> *The kind of faith it takes*
> *To climb out of this boat I'm in*
> *Onto the crashing waves*

To step out of my comfort zone
Into the realm of the unknown where Jesus is
And he's holding out his hand

But the waves are calling out my name
And they laugh at me

The lyrics to the "Voice of Truth" didn't come overnight. They marinated in me through years of struggle with constant doubts and questions like: "I know this Scripture is true. I know what the pastor just said is true. But I don't know what to do with this. I've got to start sharing my faith. Why does all this stuff never leave church with me? I'm so sick of myself."

The idea behind the "Voice of Truth" was to depict just one more day in a believer's life at church. She's sitting there and hearing the pastor say, "God has a plan for you. You are here on purpose." And yet the believer feels trapped in fear, doubt, and in sin—the kind that Hebrews says so easily entangles us.

What Hebrews is saying to that believer is that she is not running her race. She hasn't even started. She's stuck at the starting line, wrapped up in her own stuff, and it's where she'll one day die, still having not run the race.

Conversely, in 2 Timothy 4:7 Paul says, "I have fought the good fight. I have finished the race. I have kept the faith." How did he keep the faith? By doing whatever Jesus told him to do. He listened. He obeyed. He ran the greatest of races. God's nudge is his starter's pistol to let us know it's time to go. It's time to run the race.

NEXT STEPS
___

✝ Where do I see myself in this?

✝ What is the next step God is showing me?

✝ My prayer:

HOLDING BACK

"Choose a man for yourselves, and let him come down to me."
1 SAMUEL 17:8

I WROTE "What If I Gave Everything" on our new album as the prequel to the "Voice of Truth." At first I called the song "Still Standing Here" because the song starts with the question all believers face at one time or another: "Why am I still standing here? I know better. I know I should get moving."

It's fun to enjoy the aftermath of going to the theater to see *Lord of the Rings* or *Gladiator* or any movie with epic battles. You're sitting there in that huge moment at the end when the screen goes black, the coolest song ever cranks up, and the credits begin to roll. Suddenly, you're ready to conquer the world. I like watching men leave the theater after those kinds of movies. They stand up looking stiff and walk down the aisle with their chests poked out like, "Excuse me, I can't get my arms through the crowd because they're so massive and stick out so far. I'll just have to walk sideways down the steps."

All of us men are that way. We just sat on our butts for two and a half hours, ate Starburst Minis, and drank a Coke, yet we act like we lived the movie we just watched. We didn't do anything. We were the audience to somebody else's adventure. But I believe those moments are evidence of our spirits shouting from within: "That needs to be me! That *must* be me!"

I encountered those feelings over and over when I began to learn how to follow God and do the very next thing. It happened all through high school and college and even when I entered ministry. I couldn't help but think, "Nobody in church is actually doing what they're saying. It's time. Let's do this."

> **Those moments are evidence of our spirits shouting from within: "That needs to be me!"**

That's why the "Voice of Truth" includes the lyric: "Oh, what I would do to have the kind of faith it takes…" It's the cry of every person who yearns to be the hero of a story. It's the cry of every believer who wants to live for Jesus.

And it's why "What If I Gave Everything" asks the simple question we all long to answer. *God, what if I stopped holding back from you?*

Next Steps

✝ Where do I see myself in this?

✝ What is the next step God is showing me?

✝ My prayer:

Longing to Be the Hero

"For the battle is the Lord's, and he will give you into our hand."
1 SAMUEL 17:47

HAVE YOU SPENT most of your life longing to be the hero, sword raised high and running to the battle? I know I have. I also know I've looked more like the guy hiding behind the tree, hoping no one sees me watching with one eye.

David was the youngest of the sons of Jesse when his dad sent him to carry food to his three oldest brothers in Israel's army camp. When he heard Goliath taunt the Israelites and rail against God, he was offended. So he acted. It was a mammoth exercise in faith and trust in the Lord, and here's the bottom line that we're afraid to face:

> **It's part of human nature to want to be the hero.**

David loved the Lord more than he loved his own life.

Every time you hear the story of David and Goliath, it's easy to go into epic movie mode, fantasize about yourself in David's sandals, and think, "Yeah. Let's do this." It's part of human nature to want to be the hero. Surely, the entire Israelite army felt the same way. Imagine those soldiers sitting in that valley, clenching their teeth and seething as they watched a menacing giant come out twice a day for 40 days, a total of 80 times, and curse God. They all wanted to be the hero but felt utterly defeated by their own fear. Then some kid half their age walks up, hears the giant's boasts only one time, and immediately reacts: "Oh, nay nay. Did he say what I think he just said? Ain't happening."

The soldiers hated David at first. His own brothers mocked him: "What are you doing here? You're just here to see the battle." But deep down inside, each of them thought: "Why am I not the one stepping forward like this? Why am I not running down to that valley to meet the giant like David?"

The famous evangelist D. L. Moody once said, "The world has yet to see what God can do with a man fully consecrated to him." It was his way of issuing believers a simple challenge:

Do we love the Lord more than we love our own lives?

Next Steps

✝ Where do I see myself in this?

✝ What is the next step God is showing me?

✝ My prayer:

The Line

"For he is a chosen instrument of mine to carry my name...."
Acts 9:15

IN MY MOST honest moments, I've had to look at Jesus and say, "I'm so afraid of what it might cost to follow you. I'd walk by faith if I could just get these feet to move."

It reminds me of the story of the Apostle Paul's escape from Damascus in Acts 9. All of our lives reflect Paul's life to a point:

Lost, Saved, Attacked…. The Line.

All believers once were lost and then were saved by God's grace. All believers have suffered in some way for their faith—whether it was spiritual attack or outright persecution. All have come up to what I call "The Line." Paul had the same experience.

Paul was lost, just like we were. Sure, his was a dramatic and eventful life. He was famous for his religious fervor and rigid adherence to his faith. Then he got saved, just like we did. Granted, his salvation was probably the most dramatic in history, but all believers are just as saved as Paul.

Paul went away and spent time with the Lord and grew. When he publicly stepped out into his new faith, his old

Jewish friends wanted to kill him. The next thing he knew, Paul found himself in a basket being lowered down a high wall in the middle of the night.

Can you imagine climbing in that basket and not being able to see a thing? Men are literally watching every gate, waiting to kill you. But in your basket, all you can hear is that rope stretching and that basket creaking as you strain to hear every voice and every threatening sound. There aren't a whole lot of ways to defend yourself in a basket.

This moment of fear and uncertainty is where most believers think, "It's time for me to hop off the Jesus bus. This ain't working." As soon as attack comes, most of us decide we're out. How many times has God called me out for a specific reason only to watch me shrink back when it got tough? Our baskets creak and our ropes strain and we tell ourselves, "Uh oh, I can't do this. Not even God is helping me."

I don't want to look back some day to a life that never stepped across the line. It's like God walked Paul up to that basket, drew a line right in front of him, and said, "OK, you've got two choices. You can stop here, and you can come to church every Sunday and sing every word off of every screen and say 'Amen' to every sermon point and highlight every verse of emphasis in your Bible. And you'll be with me some day. You're already mine. Or…

"Or you can step across this line and completely abandon yourself to me and trust me with what comes next." And Paul moved his right foot ahead of his left and did the very next thing.

Next Steps

✝ Where do I see myself in this?

✝ What is the next step God is showing me?

✝ My prayer:

OTHER PEOPLE

"You will seek me and find me, when you seek me with all your heart."
JEREMIAH 29:13

I MENTIONED HENRY BLACKABY'S powerful book *Experiencing God* earlier. That study changed my life when I was 22 years old. I was a brand new youth pastor and bought the curriculum for my students because it had a cool cover. It depicted Moses and the burning bush, and I thought the fiery scene looked cutting edge for Christian studies at the time. That's about where I was in my walk with the Lord—cool covers.

But when I started learning ideas like *God is always at work around us* and *the key to experiencing God is to find where he is at work and join him there*, scales fell from my eyes. It's pretty easy to tell where God is making a difference, if we're looking for it. When we see what he is doing around us, sometimes doing the very next thing involves just joining him there.

Yet I also learned that every new truth God teaches us in his Word will bring us to a crisis of belief. Will we choose to take God at his Word, or will we allow old thought patterns to drown out what the Lord is trying to show us and the new opportunities he wants to bring? What we believe is borne out in how we respond to a crisis of belief—in what we do.

When it comes to the very next thing, all of us are in different stages of *next*. We're all at different stages of these major areas:

✝ Understanding who God is
✝ Seeing ourselves the way God sees us
✝ Realizing where we easily stumble
✝ Understanding that God can and will take us right where we are
✝ Discerning what we should do next

It involves maturing past the "forgive-me-help-me" stage and turning our focus on others to see people as God sees them.

When we soak in God's Word and stop dwelling so much on ourselves, we begin to move into the next stage of maturity of focusing on other people. When our very next thing involves other people, we're headed in the right direction.

NEXT STEPS

☩ Where do I see myself in this?

☩ What is the next step God is showing me?

☩ My prayer:

The Very Next Thing

SUNDAY PRELUDE

My band Casting Crowns gets to travel a lot, which is fun. We see all kinds of interesting places and meet all kinds of people. Some of the most fun acquaintances are "runners" and volunteers at our concerts. The runners are the people who drive us around the venue grounds or around town or do errands to help us, because once the bus driver stops at our concert location, he goes to bed and we're stuck. We don't know what the front of any arena looks like. We know the loading dock. We know the areas where our kids ride their scooters. We know the dumpster. And that's it. We'll be in a town and say, "Oh, yeah, I recognize that…smell."

One year, I met a guy hanging around the venue in a large city in the Midwest. I could tell right away he wasn't a runner. He was a friend of the promoter. He seemed distinguished, a bit stoic. We needed to go somewhere, and the promoter looked at his very serious-looking friend.

"Do you mind driving them?" the promoter said.

"Sure."

As the serious guy drove, I struck up a conversation with

him. After getting his name, I did what everybody else does. I asked him what he does for a living. He told me he worked for a national chain of stores.

"I'm in charge of security," he said.

"Cool. Which store?"

"All of 'em."

Well now. This is going to be fun.

You never have to wonder what I'm thinking. It just sort of flies out.

"So, um, got any stories?" I asked.

All you have to do is go to any large store around midnight and you can find some stories—stories you never could imagine. Mr. Security had been formal with us, but he loosened up a little at my question.

"I'll tell you one," he said, "if you don't tell anybody."

I was like, "No problem. Hit me."

So here's his story.

His chain has a particularly large store in a midwestern metropolis. Before he was the head of all security for his chain, he was the head of one of its megastores in this metropolis. The store is so large that it has about 800 employees and is basically a small city. Here's his story:

One day Mr. Security is summoned to the video room.

"We have a problem," one of his video guys says. "I'm trying to figure out what's going on."

Mr. Security stares at the video monitor. He sees shoppers milling around and begins to sort through them to find a shoplifter. He can tell you a thousand stories about someone trying to shove a flat-screen TV up her skirt.

"Everything looks normal," he says. "I don't see anything."

"Sir, we're not talking about the shoppers," the video guy says. "We're talking about the workers. Watch the workers."

The security chief refocuses on the employees in the video. He watches a young man in a worker's vest casually looking around as he walks. Then the worker walks around a display of clothes…and disappears.

"Roll that back," Mr. Security says.

He watches it again. And the guy walks around the clothes rack, and he never comes out.

"What's going on with that?" the chief asks. The video guy shrugs.

They cue up other angles. Same thing. The employee walks around the clothes display and vanishes.

Mr. Security decides to pick the right moment to trail one of the employees they suspect as he walks to the clothing area. Mr. Security is incredulous as he watches the clothes rack easily part as the employee walks through it. So Mr. Security decides to follow the employee into the clothes. He pauses at the rack, somewhere between sizes medium and large. He steps into the rack, through the clothes….

It was like Narnia. Mr. Security walked through the clothes into another world.

The employees at this megastore had taken a bunch of

display shelving and built a room. It measured 1,400 square feet. I typed the dimensions into my phone as he said it. Yes— 1,400 square feet. It had couches. Chairs. A television. A video game console.

The security chief trailed the employee right into a secret room. One guy was sitting on a couch and eating cereal. I can just see the worker's face as he brings a spoonful of Cheerios to his mouth, milk dripping back into the bowl, and looks up to see Mr. Security. The spoon freezes in mid-air. His eyes widen. He glances down at his bowl and back up at Mr. Security.

"I'm fired, right?"

"Yes. Yes, you are. Narnia is closed."

I kept asking Mr. Security questions about the moment he nailed them. At different times throughout the day, about 100 employees walked through the clothes rack. And all 100 lost their jobs for coming to work, clocking in, going to their den of comfort, and staying there much of the day. I couldn't wrap my mind around the scale of what it took to pull off such a charade, but I also couldn't help but think of how familiar the story felt to me personally.

It's amazing what kinds of rooms we build. It's even more amazing that we think we'll never be seen.

Key Passages of the Week: GALATIANS 5:16-26; JOHN 4:1-26; ACTS 8

BIG THINGS FOR GOD

Walk by the Spirit, and you will not gratify the desires of the flesh.
GALATIANS 5:16

WHENEVER MOST BELIEVERS read through Scripture, we grasp it, take it to heart, and believe it. We're just not sure where our lives meet up with it.

For instance, I know I need to trust God with my life. That's a big, giant concept. I want to be on fire; I want to be all in; I want to do whatever it takes; I want to cross the line. I want to measure up to these grand, ambitious slogans that capture what I know is true.

We all believe it, and we all want it. We're just not sure what we're supposed to do with it. We're not sure what following God looks like from where we are. We have an idea of this awesome walk with Jesus "out there" somewhere, but we're looking for the bridge to get over to it. Exactly what does following Jesus look like?

> **Serving God isn't this giant dream about something that will happen a year from now.**

It's just doing the very next thing he says. The. Very. Next. Thing. Serving God isn't this giant dream about something that will happen a year from now. It's not a goal he's going to have you fulfill in a month. It's right now.

"Big things for God" is not something you do after you graduate or move on to the next position or get a promotion. "Big things for God" is the person sitting next to you right now. God put breath in your lungs to talk to that person, and you can do something right now.

The very next thing is the act of kindness you put off last week. Do it now—all in the name of Jesus. It's the phone call you need to make, the note you need to send, the meal you need to provide, the pat on the back you need to give, the hard work you need to put in, the hospital visit you need to make, the bill you need to pay, the Scripture you need to quote in love, the forgiveness you need to grant, the forgiveness you need to seek.

We can make a relationship with Jesus too complicated by dwelling on non-essentials. Following God is just the very next word of love that you need to speak to somebody, to the very next broken heart that needs to be encouraged. Ministry isn't limited to Sundays. It's not on a stage. It's not with certain gifts by certain people with certain personalities and a microphone. It's you, where you are, doing the next thing God tells you to do.

NEXT STEPS

✝ Where do I see myself in this?

✝ What is the next step God is showing me?

✝ My prayer:

THE ACTS LIFE

If we live by the Spirit, let us also keep in step with the Spirit.

GALATIANS 5:25

WE TEND TO LIVE in abstract terms—big, grandiose dreams and ideas—but the book of Acts always seems to put feet on the ground and words in people's mouths. An Acts life means your hands are touching someone else. You're moving. You're doing.

Unless your faith has a book of Acts, it's just head knowledge. Unless you can give away your faith, it's not your faith. In other words, you show you have faith by giving it away, by sharing it with others through word and deed. Sometimes the deed is easier to share than the word, but people will listen when you speak truth in love, especially after your acts show you love them.

People will listen when you speak truth in love, especially after your acts show you love them.

In a sense, the book of Acts made what we believe about Jesus real. The early believers staked their lives on the truth of the gospel and proved it with their actions. The disciples' faithfulness in the face of death and overwhelming persecution—when they were in a position to know whether what they believed was true—is strong testimony to the truth of Scripture's claims. Otherwise, all of that stuff in the Gospels happened and a guy died and it was over.

I've had believers tell me, "I get what you're saying. I know I need to honor God with my life. I know I need to stop doing things that hurt me and grieve the Holy Spirit. I know I need to be all in for him. I just don't know what I'm supposed to do. I need to know what to do."

When believers don't see the next step, they become defeated and stale. One hindrance from acting now is the idea that we're not worthy. Of course we aren't. We're so unworthy that God sent his Son to die in order to get us back into fellowship with him. How could we ever make up for that? It's impossible, so scratch "deserve grace" off your list of things to do. Just be grateful for it and let it fuel you to watch and listen for what he wants to do with you next. Pray, open your heart, and watch where he is at work. Then show your faith is real by diving in.

You surrendered your life to Jesus, right? So what's keeping you from surrendering your next moment?

NEXT STEPS

✝ Where do I see myself in this?

✝ What is the next step God is showing me?

✝ My prayer:

PERFECT ROOMS

"Whoever drinks of the water that I will give him will never be thirsty again."
JOHN 4:14

THE SAMARITAN WOMAN whom Jesus meets at the well has a knack for keeping everything in its place. Verse 9 says Jews had no association with Samaritans, so she was stunned when Jesus spoke to her. She thinks she knows where everything belongs, and she most certainly knows her place. She even knows Jesus' place—or at least she thinks she does. But for some reason this scene isn't playing out like she anticipated. She looks at Jesus and thinks, "Why are you even talking to me?"

It becomes clear she's been around religion. She knows Jews worship in Jerusalem and Samaritans worship on Mount Gerizim. That's just the way it is. But she's also made some terrible life choices. As a result, she's taken her spiritual life and put it in its place and her private life and put it in its place as well.

She comes to draw her water at the hottest part of the day to stay away from the rest of the women who visit the well in the cool of the morning. The townspeople know she's been married five times and is now living with a man who is not her husband. No doubt, the people of her community have come up with some labels to describe her. She's tired of all the whispers, so she's decided to keep her neighbors over there…and herself over here. Everything is in its perfect little place, but suddenly Jesus messes up her organization. Like Mr. Security in the earlier story, Jesus walks through her clothes rack and into her make-believe world.

Do you remember the first time Jesus walked into one of your little rooms? You had it all separated out:

These are my church friends. These are my Friday night friends. And these are my work friends.

This is my worship life. And this is my entertainment life.

He wants you to be all his at all places and all times.

This is how I act around this crowd, and this is how I act around those guys.

Do you have a place to fit each little thing neatly in your life? Have you worked diligently to construct your perfect rooms and to warp reality like the woman at the well or Mr. Security's workers?

Jesus so wants you to do the very next thing for him that he'll go out his way to meet you. He wants to remind you to tear down all the walls you've built. He wants you to be all his at all places and all times. And aren't you tired of carrying such heavy loads in the heat of the day?

NEXT STEPS

✝ Where do I see myself in this?

✝ What is the next step God is showing me?

✝ My prayer:

THE KNOWING SMILE

"With man this is impossible, but with God all things are possible."
MATTHEW 19:26

IT'S AMAZING HOW people throughout Scripture react when Jesus steps into their little rooms. Even those who think they expect it are caught off guard. For instance, no one in the rich young ruler's shoes would've ever approached Jesus before calculating exactly how the scene should unfold.

In his society, the rich young ruler was "in." Not only was he part of the in-crowd on earth, but also he was sure to make it to heaven. His culture believed that wealth was a sign of God's favor. So he was convinced he was about to curry favor from this Jesus, the deeply spiritual teacher and miracle-worker creating all the buzz.

He walks up to Jesus and his large group of disciples and asks, "What must I do to follow you?" He's thinking to himself, "Look at me. Everyone wants to be me. I can't wait to hear your reaction. Go ahead and validate me, good sir...."

Jesus says, "Keep this commandment, and this one, and this one." The rich young guy acts stoked and claims he's kept them all. Many scholars believe that Jesus listed out the particular commandments that the young man would know he had violated most.

"OK," Jesus says with a knowing smile. "Just sell everything you have, give to the poor, and let's rock."

Uh oh.

Jesus steps right into the rich young ruler's most precious room, and the Scriptures says the young man walked away sorrowful. Jesus will never cease to step into our rooms. He refuses to let us continue to construct a world of false assurances. The rich young ruler walked away sorrowful because he discovered walking with Jesus isn't about a to-do list that we can accomplish but about abandoning ourselves. It's about acknowledging that we have no rights. We are not our own. We've been bought at the greatest price ever paid, and out of gratitude we should love and serve the one who died for us.

> **Walking with Jesus isn't about a to-do list that we can accomplish but about abandoning ourselves.**

Next Steps

✝ Where do I see myself in this?

✝ What is the next step God is showing me?

✝ My prayer:

GOD'S TIMETABLE

And he rose and went.
ACTS 8:27

THE EVANGELIST PHILIP provides one of the Bible's most shining examples of doing the very next thing for Jesus. Moment by moment, the Holy Spirit tells Philip what to do and he does it.

"Go walk down that desert road."

That's all Philip knows, so he starts walking.

"Go run up to that chariot."

That's all he hears, so he starts running.

God doesn't tell him any more than the next step. But even before he tells Philip to walk down the desert road, God tells him to leave the biggest, coolest thing he's ever been a part of in Samaria. Philip is seeing revival, even revolution, in hearts and in society, and the Holy Spirit says, "OK, I want you to leave all this and go down that desert road."

Wait. What?

Remember, God's timetable doesn't match ours. His ways are higher than our ways, and his thoughts are higher than our thoughts (Isaiah 55:9). Sometimes we'll think it makes little sense to do what God is leading us to do, and many times we'll never know the results of our actions.

How long did Philip walk down that desert road? We don't know. We just know that God told him to walk, and he walked. Was it 15 minutes? Was it an hour? Was it a day? Did it take him a month to get where he was going? He just walked, and that's all he knew to do. How many of us find ourselves there? If God asks us to take a step, we can rest in the fact that he knows where it will lead.

Sometimes we'll think it makes little sense to do what God is leading us to do.

The end of Philip's obedience ought to encourage us. He leads a trusted official of the Ethiopian queen's court to the Lord and baptizes him. The Ethiopian is perhaps the first convert from the continent of Africa, and he's headed home and taking the gospel with him.

God will handle the compounding interest of our obedience if we'll only heed his Word and his voice. "And let us not grow weary while doing good, for in due season we shall reap if we do not lose heart" (Galatians 6:9).

NEXT STEPS

✝ Where do I see myself in this?

✝ What is the next step God is showing me?

✝ My prayer:

THE SIMPLEST MESSAGE

"Truly, truly, I say to you, whoever believes in me will also do the works that I do;
and greater works than these will he do, because I am going to the Father."

JOHN 14:12

DOING THE VERY next thing Jesus says isn't mysterious. It isn't some ethereal, mystical exercise.

You won't have to walk around cupping your hands behind your ears as if you'll hear something. You probably won't hear him audibly. Rather, his "still small voice" (1 Kings 19:12) will prick your heart with a thought. He will bend your desires and thoughts in a certain direction. He will speak to your heart through Scripture. He will arrange circumstances to make clear what to do next.

Why did the early Church demonstrate such radical obedience as recorded in the book of Acts? Was it just because some of them had actually lived with Jesus? It had to be more than that, because the disciples abandoned Jesus at his arrest. Instead, I think the Church was at its healthiest because it had a singularity of message and purpose.

These days, we come to church and are barraged with how to discover our spiritual gifts or obtain financial peace or be a good parent or join the choir or teach a class or go on a mission trip. I'm in favor of all of those things, but maybe the early Church was so effective because it had one clear message:

Know Christ and make him known.

Jesus told them, "I'm going up to get everything ready. You guys go make some disciples, and I'll be back soon."

And they were like, "OK."

From then on, their days began, unfolded, and ended on behalf of a Lord they knew was resurrected. The Jesus they abandoned was now the source and object of their abandonment. Everything stemmed from the message that was given them in the gospel. Today, it seems as if we dwell on our lives, our goals, our dreams, and our plans—and whether we can get the gospel to fit into those things.

The Jesus they abandoned was now the source and object of their abandonment.

We will do the very next thing only when we discover that the gospel is life itself. When we do, the very next thing is not really even an action. It's a natural reaction.

NEXT STEPS

✝ Where do I see myself in this?

✝ What is the next step God is showing me?

✝ My prayer:

One Step Away

SUNDAY PRELUDE

NOT LONG AGO, I came across a website that compiles photos taken at exactly the wrong time—or exactly the *right* time, depending on your sense of humor.

These photos capture the element of surprise (or impending doom) at its finest. In one photo, a guy in the stands at a baseball game is getting hit in the jaw by a bat that flew out of the batter's hands. In another photo, a whole wedding party stands on a dock just as it is collapsing. The bridesmaids are starting to react in horror, but the bride doesn't realize what's happening yet. She's standing there with a beaming smile that says, "This is the best day of my life." Giggle. Giggle.

One photo shows a young woman at a concert. She's sitting on a guy's shoulders and appearing to have a great time. The only problem is that she's oblivious to the large cup and long stream of fluid someone has thrown directly toward the back of her head. Impact is approximately T-minus 0.3 seconds.

Let's use our imagination with this photo.

We'll call this woman Sarah. She has a good life and even

thinks her boyfriend is about to pop the question any day now. But today is her birthday, and she's having the roughest day ever. Sarah is in a dead-end job. She's still hurting from burning herself with her curling iron and then breaking a nail while changing a flat tire on the interstate on the way to work. She works all day staring at spreadsheets on a computer screen in her cubicle. She's not sure if anyone knows it's her birthday because no one has said a word. Even her parents haven't called. Her boyfriend says he has to work late into the night. When she looks at her phone during break, everyone else's photos on Instagram are awesome. She feels like her day couldn't get much worse.

But just as Sarah is stepping into the weekly meeting she hates most, her coworkers throw open the conference room door and scream, "Surprise!" The next thing she knows, Sarah is picking confetti out of her hair, blowing out candles, and staring into the excited face of her friend from the cubicle next door.

"Happy Birthday! We all pitched in and got you a little something." The friend hands her two tickets to that night's concert by her favorite band.

"Oh, my gosh. I never could have afforded this! This is going to be so awesome!" Sarah says.

And all is well with the world again.

"You guys are the greatest," Sarah says. "This is going to be the best…day…ever."

Sarah's boyfriend manages to get off work early when he

hears about the tickets. Her day is picking up more steam. Sarah and her beau arrive early to make their way closer to the stage.

And to think Sarah was certain this was going to be the worst week ever. She was going to be alone in her little rotten cubicle for the rest of the week, squinting through the faulty fluorescent light flickering on and off above her head. But now her birthday is nothing short of spectacular. She only has one complaint.

"I just can't see," Sarah says to her boyfriend.

"Climb on," he says, and throws her up on his shoulders. Ahh. Much better now. This is a whole new world. She's right in front of the band. She's watching them. Oh my, and now they see her! She is absolutely certain the lead singer just smiled her way!

"Did you see that? They're looking right at me, man!" she screams.

Sarah is in her groove now, swaying to the music, singing and dancing the night away. Suddenly she looks around and notices what looks like a press photographer. She turns toward him just as he aims the lens at her. The thought streaks through her mind: "Wow, if he posts this somewhere, I want to see this moment, because this…this is the life."

She sees the camera flash….

And then 48 fluid ounces and a very large cup smash into the back of her head.

Sarah lunges forward, wrenching the neck of her

boyfriend, and now he's yelling in pain. As she tumbles to the ground, Sarah drops her purse, lands on it, and breaks her phone. She bloodies her elbow and bumps her head. When she finally scrambles to her feet, she stands stiffly with her arms away from her soaked body and screams.

"Who did this?"

Dozens of people point at a guy 20 feet away, and Sarah's boyfriend stands up and realizes this could get nasty as he asks himself, "Oh boy, what am I going to do now? I've got to be the guy that defends her honor. I really don't want to do this, but she's my lady. Here goes nothing."

Sarah pulls her matted hair away from her eyes just in time to see her boyfriend rolling around with some guy on the ground.

Other guys in the crowd pile on, and the melee grows. Sarah is dumbstruck.

"Good gosh, he has an anger problem," she thinks. "What if we have kids? Is he going to be this quick-tempered with us? I don't think this is the guy for me after all."

When order is restored, Sarah promptly walks up to her deranged boyfriend and breaks up with him while the police are handcuffing him.

"But I did this for you!" he yells as the cops tug him away. Sarah squishes home alone, still soaking wet, cold, and stinking from whatever was in that cup. She lies in bed, wipes away a tear, and sighs.

"My life is officially toast."

As Sarah scrolls through Facebook on her shattered phone screen, looking at everyone else's wonderful lives, her thumb freezes on the screen. She sees a link from the local newspaper to a story about a fight at the concert. And right above the headline she sees her perfectly timed snapshot from the photographer. The cup and its stream are right behind her. And then a thought hits her harder than the cup ever did.

That one moment changed everything. Nothing will ever be the same, and her heart aches to go back. If only she could have a do-over.

"All I had to do was this," she thinks, moving her head slightly to the right. "If I had ducked, life would be perfect right now. But now I'm stuck. Anything I do from this point forward is Plan B. Everybody in the world sees this and knows what a loser I am now. I was supposed to spend my life with this guy I just discovered has anger issues, and for the rest of my life I was supposed to tell the story of the best birthday ever at the best concert ever. I can never get back to that moment right there in that photo. And now I'm here."

That's Sarah's story. Forgive the hyperbole, but most of us can say we've experienced similar feelings about pivotal moments in our lives. Haven't we all wondered if somewhere along the way we settled for Plan B?

If we see life as Plan B—or even Plan C or D—we'll never find the abundant peace and joy God promises. The good news is that the antidote to the kind of regret and remorse that paralyzes our hopes and dreams is part of God's plan for us to do the very next thing he says. The real turning point can come anywhere along the way.

The antidote is this: We're all just one step away from surrender. One step away from coming home.

Key Passages of the Week: LUKE 15:11-32; JAMES 1:19-25

60

A NEW BEGINNING

He began to be in need.
LUKE 15:14

SOMETIMES CHRISTIANS FEEL frozen because they believe that to follow God best, they need to get back to an earlier, more spiritual version of themselves. But we can follow God from right where we are.

Many of us remember a time when we walked more closely with the Lord. We can even find ourselves comfortably numb in a state of inertia, seemingly unable to move forward because we're allowing something in our past to hold us back. Maybe we committed blatant sin. Maybe we're struggling to forgive someone who hurt us. Maybe we're angry with someone or something. Too often, consciously or subconsciously, we resign ourselves to the thought that our lives are probably not what they were supposed to be and it's all Plan B from here. How do you have hope in Plan B?

A better question is: How do you follow God when life doesn't work out exactly as you had planned? What do you do after a failure that was your own doing or a surprise that was out of your control?

Maybe something happened and you can't detach from it

and you're always thinking about it. The thought is always there, lurking just under the surface, forever grabbing some of your hard drive space and sapping you of hope and confidence. The thought goes something like this: "There was a time when my faith was really strong and I walked with God, but I'm just not there anymore. I could never get back there. I've tried to get back to that point but I just can't."

You don't have to. Jesus is willing to start all over with you from where you are right now. If we were good enough to please God on our own, we would've never needed a Savior in the first place.

If we were good enough to please God on our own, we would've never needed a Savior in the first place.

Allow God to do what he's trying to do. He's trying to tell you to let your past rest in his sea of forgetfulness. Don't allow lies and guilt over "these things I've done, these places I've gone, and these things I've seen" derail the most important relationship you could ever have. Jesus is so much bigger than your failure.

NEXT STEPS

☩ Where do I see myself in this?

☩ What is the next step God is showing me?

☩ My prayer:

CRUSTY HEARTS

"I will arise and go to my father ...."
LUKE 15:18

ONE OF MY favorite lines in the Bible refers to the prodigal son and is found in Luke 15:17. It says, "But when he came to himself..."

Here's a young man who has squandered his inheritance on partying and finds himself at just about the lowest point a Jewish boy could go. He has a job feeding pigs—considered unclean animals by Jews—and he is so hungry that he wants to eat their nasty leftovers. He's come a long way from the time when he wanted the father's stuff but didn't want the father.

God is faithful to shape us through trial and our error.

We should remember that sometimes God uses pain to peel back our layers and soften our crusty hearts. First Peter 3:17 confirms that God not only allows us to suffer but even wills it. His crucible can be intense but is always fair, always true, and is designed to mold us into the image of Christ. The prodigal son had to learn the hard way, as many of us do, and God is faithful to shape us through trial and our error.

Never believe the mistaken notion that "God will never give you anything you can't handle." That's an errant belief, twisted out of 1 Corinthians 10:13, which refers to temptation, not trial. God most certainly will give you something you cannot handle. If you believe God is sovereign, then you know that nothing happens outside of his control. He either brings or allows everything that touches you, so either way it's his will.

It just may be God's will that we get cancer, and I know firsthand that you can't handle cancer on your own. God may allow you to lose a job. He may even allow you to lose a loved one. But amid our deepest struggles—whether self-inflicted or out of our control—he is faithful and just not only to cleanse us of all unrighteousness (1 John 1:9), but also to restore, confirm, strengthen, and establish us after we have suffered a little while (1 Peter 5:10).

The Lord knows our breaking points. He knows what it will take for us to come to ourselves. Be sure that he will allow us to get there. But be just as sure that he's always ready for us to come home.

NEXT STEPS

✝ Where do I see myself in this?

✝ What is the next step God is showing me?

✝ My prayer:

GREATER THAN

He does not deal with us according to our sins,
nor repay us according to our iniquities.
PSALM 103:10

GOD FILLED THE BIBLE with people just as bad or even worse than we are, which should assure us that we can follow him from where we are. Their stories remind us we're always just one step away from surrender.

A lot of us somewhere along the line have decided, "I think I've failed too many times for God to use me. How many times can one person go to the altar? How many times can I get down on my knees and beg forgiveness and say I'm never going to do it again? How many times can I say I want to walk with Jesus and live for him? How many second chances are there, for crying out loud?"

And how many times do we stop and start before we finally decide for ourselves, "This whole Jesus deal doesn't work. I've tried that already. All the stuff that the pastor says and all of these books say are just not for me because I can't do it. I tried it, and it didn't work. It's too late. I'm not good enough."

Show me where you can find that in the Bible. There's just

not a verse for it. God doesn't love you because you're good; he loves you because he's good.

You can't give up on pursuing God because you're frustrated that life hasn't followed your agenda. The Bible is full of losers—guys who did a bunch of wrong things and a bunch of things wrong. And why did God do that? Why did he use them? The same reason he takes someone like me—struggling with dyslexia and ADD so badly that I often can't remember the words to my own songs—and puts me onstage in front of people. The same reason why he takes people who have blown it in every conceivable fashion and puts them in charge of ministries all around the world.

He does it to show the world his surpassing power and glory, to point people to him by using the Less Than to show that he is Greater Than.

Many of us have done more stupid things since we've been saved than we did before we were saved. Some of our biggest mistakes in life have come after Jesus covered us in his shed blood. It doesn't matter how far you've gone. Mercy says you don't have to keep running down the road you're on. Love has never met a lost cause.

God knows we're going to blow it a million and one times. The proper response to his inexhaustible grace is a melted heart of gratitude. Sometimes the very next thing is to say, "Lord, I'm sorry, forgive me. Help me lay down my old chains. Help me take up my new name."

NEXT STEPS

✝ Where do I see myself in this?

✝ What is the next step God is showing me?

✝ My prayer:

JOHN 4:27-42

THIS TIME IT'S DIFFERENT

"Come, see a man who told me all that I ever did. Can this be the Christ?"
JOHN 4:29

IF EVER ANYONE figured they could never have a fresh start with God, it had to be the woman at the well. We've already seen how Jesus walked into all of her little rooms. One of the coolest verses in all of Scripture shows how she responds.

Verse 28 says, "So the woman left her water jar and went away into town and said to the people...."

Wait. The town? She left the water jar—what she thought was her source of fulfillment—and went to talk to the people in the town? The town she's trying to stay away from? The people who want nothing to do with her and from whom she hides? She goes straight to those same people to tell them what? "Come see a man who told me everything I've ever done." Don't we know that they pretty much know everything she's ever done? Does something look strange here?

It's almost like she's saying to her neighbors, "I know you guys know my past, but Jesus just told me everything I've ever done even though he had never met me before. He stepped into my room and showed me all the darkness in my life, but it was different when he said it.

"He said, 'It's OK. You can follow me from here.' And I believed him."

You can handle Jesus walking into your room in different ways. You can run. You can fight. You can divert. You can get all religious. You can make as big a case as you want, and that is where you'll stay. Because to leave God's will to get what you want means that you have to stay out there to keep it.

He steps into your room to show you himself.

When Jesus steps into your room to show you something that's hurting you and keeping you from him, he doesn't do it just to highlight your sin. He steps into your room to show you himself. It's to take you by the hand and lead you out. Your place is to follow him. You can follow him from devotion. You can follow him from a place of shame. You can even follow him from a place of anger or doubt. What did the father who begged Jesus to heal his son say in Mark 9:24? "Lord, I believe, but help me with my unbelief." He was saying, "This is all I have. But can you take me from here?"

Yes. Yes, he can.

Next Steps

✛ Where do I see myself in this?

✛ What is the next step God is showing me?

✛ My prayer:

JAMES 1:19-22

DOERS OF THE WORD

Receive with meekness the implanted word, which is able to save your souls.

JAMES 1:21

AMID THE GROWTH, persecution, and dispersion of the Jerusalem church, James remained its rock-steady leader until Jewish leaders trumped up charges against him and stoned him to death several decades after Jesus' crucifixion. Actually, they first took James to the pinnacle of the temple—the same pinnacle to which Satan took Jesus for the second of his three temptations (Matthew 4:5-7). There, they challenged James to deny the deity of Christ, his half-brother. When he refused, they threw him to the ground. The fall did not kill him, so they finished him off by stoning him.

Talk about your actions proving your faith. At any point, James could've disavowed Jesus and walked away without a scratch. Instead, he walked the walk after talking the talk.

> **Faith and works are not mutually exclusive but go hand-in-hand.**

Before his death, James wrote a letter to tell scattered and persecuted Christians that faith and works are not mutually exclusive but go hand-in-hand. The epistle also gives instruction on self-control: "Know this, my beloved brothers: let every person be quick to hear, slow to speak, slow to anger; for the anger of man does not produce the righteousness of God. Therefore put away all filthiness and rampant wickedness and receive with meekness the implanted word, which is able to save your souls" (James 1:19-21).

Most of us have heard or read the first part of that passage. It's practical, makes sense, and resonates with all believers. But sometimes we skim right past verse 21: "Receive with meekness the implanted word."

He's telling us to do what we already know to do. In other words, stop coming to church looking for some new thing. A lot of folks struggle with this. We want some new, deeper idea or approach. We need someone to discover a new book of the Bible so we can be interested again. James says that if believers would obey what's already been planted in us through God's Word, we'd be rocking. We wouldn't have enough room in our churches every Sunday.

Then comes the familiar verse 22: "But be doers of the word, and not hearers only, deceiving yourselves."

As you pursue Christ with your whole heart by loving him, his Word, and other people in his name, you become more like him. That is the beautiful simplicity of the gospel. There is no new thing to find or secret level to attain before you're approved to be his ambassador. Doing the very next thing Jesus asks of you makes you a doer of the Word.

NEXT STEPS

✝ Where do I see myself in this?

✝ What is the next step God is showing me?

✝ My prayer:

THE MIRROR

For he looks at himself and goes away and at once forgets what he was like.
JAMES 1:24

A MIRROR IS nothing but truth.

Even if the world's best artist drew a picture of you, something would be inaccurate. You'd say, "Oh, no, my nose isn't that big. My ears aren't that wide, my eyes aren't that close together. It looks like a Volkswagen. It doesn't look like me."

James 1:23-24 says, "For if anyone is a hearer of the word and not a doer, he is like a man who looks intently at his natural face in a mirror. For he looks at himself and goes away and at once forgets what he was like."

Hearing the Word gives us an accurate picture of who we are in Christ.

You can't argue with a mirror. It is what it is.

In the same way, a person who listens to truth but isn't a doer of truth is someone who forgets what he looks like as a Christ-follower. James says we're hearers rather than doers of the Word when we live as if we go to a mirror, run our hands through our messy hair a few times, and take off into an unkempt day. We forget what we look like, and the results are ugly.

Hearing the Word gives us an accurate picture of who we are in Christ. But if we don't do what the Word says, then it's like we've forgotten who we are. We keep going back to the mirror (the Word) for truth about who we are, and then we live like we don't know it.

Thankfully, James doesn't mince words. He offers a blunt, practical answer in the next verse: "But the one who looks into the perfect law, the law of liberty, and perseveres, being no hearer who forgets but a doer who acts, he will be blessed in his doing" (v. 25).

The answer is to be a disciple who "looks into" the perfect law of liberty, God's Word, and then acts in accordance. That means the believer looks into Scripture as though it's a mirror and says, "God, show me what needs to change. I'm all yours."

When we look at Scripture that way, not forgetting what we have heard but doing it, we honor God. We tell him we value nothing more than his shaping presence in our lives.

Scripture will stick a mirror in a believer's face as God says in a loving way, "I love you, but this is you. This is what we need to talk about and change."

When we answer, "Lord, you showed me something. I looked into your mirror and I saw it. I really need to work on that," we take that all-important initial step toward becoming doers of the Word.

NEXT STEPS

✝ Where do I see myself in this?

✝ What is the next step God is showing me?

✝ My prayer:

O My Soul

SUNDAY PRELUDE

I WAS AT a funeral when I learned I had cancer.

Gulp.

When the doctor calls to tell you that news, you don't really hear, "You have cancer." You hear, "You're going to die." No matter how the doctor communicates it, that's the message you receive. All you can think at first is, "I have cancer. If this round doesn't get me, it'll be back soon."

When I got the call, that's how I felt even though I've met cancer survivors all over the world. All I could think about was pain, chemo, and my obituary. When it hits you personally, any pragmatic ideas you've had about cancer being treatable and "not the death sentence it used to be" goes out the window. Suddenly cancer equals death. I've heard it said that it's not if you're going to get cancer but *when* you're going to get it and what kind. So I just figured it was my turn.

On Wednesday, February 11, 2015, I was at a funeral for a young man in our church. A day or two earlier, I had gone to the doctor to get checked out for acid reflux. A lot of singers battle with reflux because of how hard we strain our diaphragms. My doctor is a friend from church, so when I saw his name pop up on my silenced phone at the funeral, my heart sank. While the doctor is my friend, we don't have daily chats. I excused myself because I knew it had to be significant.

I remember walking out into the lobby thinking, "This is about to happen. I'm about to have that moment that I've been helping other people through half my life."

My instincts were right.

"There's a tumor in your kidney that is basically the size of your kidney," the doctor said. "We've got to take out the kidney."

And that's when my screaming emotions took over. *That's it. You're dead. What would you like on your tombstone?*

The funny thing is that through the years I've had friends with kidney stones, and I remember praying, "Lord, please help them feel better…and please don't ever let me get one." So while I prayed for no kidney stones, I never thought to say anything about kidney boulders. Lesson learned. Remember to keep prayers specific.

When my doctor broke the news, he quickly followed it up with some encouragement. "Mark, if you had to lay out all of the cancers on the table and pick one," he said, "this is the one you'd want." I needed about a split second.

"Is there another table? One with cake on it or something?"

He laughed. I laughed. Probably to keep from crying.

Today I'm cancer free. The doctors removed my kidney and the cancerous tumor was completely encased by the kidney. Nothing had metastasized, so all the bad little boogers stayed in one spot. No chemo. No radiation.

I have kidney disease (not cancer) in my remaining kidney. I have Stage Three kidney disease, which means I'm two stages away from needing a new kidney. Basically, it means my life has changed a great deal and I can't eat and drink all the things I used to eat and drink. I'm holding stable for now, and I can actually see improvement if I'm more disciplined in what I eat and drink.

But when you're dealing with a disease, even good news sounds like bad news. You hear things like: "Mr. Hall, the good news is that the cancer was totally enclosed in your kidney. So when we took out the kidney, we removed all of the cancer." (Pause). "If it comes back, it will be in your lung, but we should be able to get that too."

Wait. What? Can't you just stop at, "We got all the cancer"?

I remember climbing into my car after the funeral at which I learned I had cancer. I headed home feeling halfway numb until something snapped me to attention. God was speaking through a friend, Bart Millard, the singer and masterful songwriter of the band Mercy Me. In the midst of my funk, I heard a familiar sound. It was Bart's voice.

Mercy Me's song "Greater" was playing on the radio. I heard the lyric, "Greater is the one living inside of me than he who is living in the world." It met me right where I was in that moment as God reminded me, "Hey, this is new just to you. You're the only one that this is new to. I'm not surprised in the least. You're going to be OK."

Now, I still had my emotional moments later. My mind went berserk several more times in the midst of the storm. But that was the first of several lessons I learned in the coming days. I'd like to share a few of them with you in your next few coming days.

Key Passages of the Week: PSALM 42:1-11; 2 CORINTHIANS 1:3-5

THE GOD YOU KNOW

My soul thirsts for God, for the living God.
PSALM 42:2

THE NIGHT I discovered I had cancer, I sat down at the piano. That's how songwriters bleed. We bleed songs. I started writing out my feelings, and a song called "O My Soul" began to emerge. It portrays my inner turmoil and battle with myself, reminiscent of some of David's verses in the book of Psalms. One of the coolest lines ever is when David says, "Why so downcast, O my soul? Put your hope in God." He's talking to himself and asking, "What's your problem, dude? Shake it off. Trust in God. He's going to walk you through this."

The theme of much of my ministry is "Thrive." It's the name of my student ministry's Wednesday night worship service and also the name of one of our albums and a book. It has nothing to do with prosperity in a material sense. It has everything to do with thriving in our relationship with Jesus. To thrive, we must consistently dig into Scripture to establish our roots because storms are going to come. Life is going to happen. When cancer came, my storm reeled me for a minute. Yet I noticed that as crazy and out of control as life felt, all of my feelings kept slamming into something solid in me that wouldn't move. And that was my roots and my faith and what I knew to be true.

That's the origin of a special line in the song I wrote that night: "There's a place where fear has to face the God you know." There's a difference between how you feel and whom you know, and in those moments, I had to pull away from what I was feeling and remember the Jesus I know.

> **"There's a place where fear has to face the God you know."**

The same Holy Spirit whose gentle tugs prompt us to do the very next thing will also remind us that he did not give us a spirit of fear but of power, love, and self-control. (2 Timothy 1:7) But even the self-control is not of ourselves. It must be rooted in Scripture to have any efficacy and staying power. It is interesting that when Peter discusses self-control in 2 Peter 1:5-6, he lists knowledge as its building block. The way to self-control is to saturate yourself in the knowledge of Scripture.

Someday, perhaps soon, you'll hear peals of thunder on the horizon. Trouble will come. Be encouraged in this: Just remember the God you know. And be challenged in this: What are you doing to build your root system and get to know him more?

NEXT STEPS

✝ Where do I see myself in this?

✝ What is the next step God is showing me?

✝ My prayer:

GOD'S RESCUE

My soul is cast down within me; therefore I remember you.

PSALM 42:6

As **DAVID POURS** out his heart to the Lord in Psalm 42, the story has an abrupt break. You can see the little light bulb go on above his head.

"These things I remember," David says in verse 4. It's like he pauses long enough to remind himself: "OK, I know what I'm feeling, but what do I know? Let's rediscover what I know. I have to go back to who God is, what he says about himself in his Word, and what he says about me."

That's what I had to do when I heard the word "cancer." I had to go back to what I had learned through little Quiet Time devotionals and Christian songs. I had to remember the truth and encouragement poured into me by my parents, pastors, Sunday School teachers, youth workers, and friends. I heard their words over and over: "God is sovereign. He's already there, not only in the middle of this thing but also on the other side of it. He knows everything. And he's going to get you through it."

I'm 47 years old, and I've seen God move many times. I've seen healing happen. I've seen relationships restored. I've seen God bring things to conclusion that I never, ever thought would come around. At the same time, I've seen people go unhealed. And I've seen people gather around and pray for something that never happened. Even in those moments I saw that he's still worthy of my praise. God is still good even if my day was bad. It helps to remember that my next breath is an act of God's grace. Before Christ, I was dead in my sins. Dead men can't do anything, but God rescued me. I owe him my life.

> **God is still good even if my day was bad. It helps to remember that my next breath is an act of God's grace.**

Just remember in downcast times to pause and say to yourself, "These things I remember…." Then recite all the goodness of God in your life. It's an act of worship that elevates the Lord to his rightful place and places your woes in their rightful place.

NEXT STEPS

✝ Where do I see myself in this?

✝ What is the next step God is showing me?

✝ My prayer:

PSALM 42:8-11

GOD'S TRUTH

Hope in God; for I shall again praise him, my salvation and my God.

PSALM 103:10

TAKE YOUR FIST and hit your thigh a few times. That's what it sounds like when life hits God's truth.

At my darkest moments, the swell of emotions pounding my soul kept hitting something that wouldn't move. That solid object was the root system I had cultivated in my faith—the truth I had soaked into my core over years of personal Bible study and prayer. It was everything I've ever learned about who God is and what he does and how he works—and even the fact that storms do indeed come. One of Jesus' closest companions, the Apostle Peter, wrote: "Beloved, do not be surprised at the fiery trial when it comes upon you to test you, as though something strange were happening to you" (1 Peter 4:12).

> **That solid object was the root system I had cultivated in my faith — the truth I had soaked into my core.**

Examples of these kinds of trials are all through the Bible. Sometimes they go away and sometimes they don't. You can listen to whatever TV preachers you want, and they may try to sell you on sowing a seed for your special blessing, but you cannot get away from the fact that every disciple went down in smoke. Not one walked out of it unscathed, and their faith was better than mine. They knew more about Jesus. They gave their entire lives to Jesus and were beaten, stoned, and imprisoned. Life still happened to them even after they surrendered all for the Lord.

Jesus told John the Baptist: "Blessed is the one who doesn't fall away on account of me." He was telling John, "You're going to have to walk through this one."

It won't always feel good, and there will be moments where we won't like or want what happens to us. But when you've read God's truth, studied God's truth, memorized God's truth, prayed God's truth, and seen God's truth come alive in people's lives, you know for certain that God's truth is the only truth.

And that is the place where fear has to face the God you know.

NEXT STEPS

✝ Where do I see myself in this?

✝ What is the next step God is showing me?

✝ My prayer:

Right Thinking

Take every thought captive to obey Christ.
2 Corinthians 10:5

THE APOSTLE PAUL says that the weapons of our spiritual warfare are not of the flesh but instead are divine. God alone has the power to destroy the strongholds of wrong thinking and sinful attitudes.

All manner of emotions gripped me in the days after hearing my cancer diagnosis. My flesh offered up every argument imaginable. I thought, "We're the good guys, God. I'm out here living for you and singing for you. I'm not exactly playing a lot of golf these days. I'd like a day or two off every once in a while, but I've been going hard for more than a decade. And this is what I get? What's going on?"

So God was like, "OK, how about several months off?" Boom.

The next thing I knew, I was at home recuperating from surgery. When I calmed down, I realized I don't deserve the favor God has shown me.

"Let's think of it reasonably," I told myself. "I haven't exactly been the Crossfit poster child. Do I really deserve to be that blessed by my prayer to make me healthier when I eat triple bacon cheeseburgers? Of course I have cancer. I pretty much *should* have cancer. There are triathletes with cancer. If anyone should have it, I should."

The less you're in Scripture, the more you can run with your feelings. Unfortunately for my feelings, God made me a youth pastor. So, like it or not, I'm in the Word even on days when I'm at that numb place all of us sometimes find ourselves. God has infused me with his truth, and the truth just wouldn't go away even in my lowest times. The only way we'll ever be able to trust and proclaim God's promises is to know them. The only way to know them is to care for the Word of the Lord so that we abide in it.

> **The only way we'll ever be able to trust and proclaim God's promises is to know them.**

We are transformed by the renewing of our minds (Romans 12:1-2). The way we renew our minds is through God's Word. We have to read God's Word for it renew us. It is how we are transformed into the image of Christ and how we get to know him more. To know him is to love him. To love him is to serve him. And to serve him is to live for him through the very next things he brings our way.

Next Steps

✝ Where do I see myself in this?

✝ What is the next step God is showing me?

✝ My prayer:

A False Humility

So that we may be able to comfort those who are in any affliction, with the comfort with which we ourselves are comforted by God.

2 Corinthians 1:4

BEING A YOUTH PASTOR all my adult life, most of my days have been about making other people's days better. I've always been the one who came alongside the hurting friend or student and said, "I'm going to help get you get through this. Here's some Scripture for you. Here's some encouragement. Let's walk through this together." So cancer turned the tables on me. Now it was my turn to hear from other people.

And I didn't like it one bit.

I just didn't want to deal with people. I didn't want to be comforted. I didn't want a bunch of people hovering around and patting me on the back with well-worn phrases like, "Well, brother, it's always darkest before the dawn." I didn't want to be sent a hundred different inspirational memes on Twitter and Instagram. I just didn't want to be the hurting guy. I found it much more comfortable being the comforter rather than the comforted.

I rationalized it by telling myself that I didn't want everybody to have to struggle for what to say, because it's human nature to think you have to try to fix things. But it was a false humility. It took a minute for me to realize that every one of those feelings boiled down to one thing.

Pride.

Whatever your storm, however deep your heartache, remember that you need to let the Church be the Church and let people do what they do. The most challenging part of being a disciple of Christ is humbling our hearts to acknowledge our neediness. It's very difficult for our prideful hearts to receive anything. We like to give because it empowers us. It makes us feel good. It may even make us feel like we're better or holier than others.

> **The most challenging part of being a disciple of Christ is humbling our hearts to acknowledge our neediness.**

Just as we must receive God's grace to be his child, we also must learn to taste the grace of others who love us. Scripture calls the Church the body of Christ. That means when we receive from the Church, we receive from his body. I'll take that every time.

NEXT STEPS

✝ Where do I see myself in this?

✝ What is the next step God is showing me?

✝ My prayer:

2 Corinthians 1:5

——

Just Be There

Blessed be the God and Father of our Lord Jesus Christ, the Father of mercies and God of all comfort.

2 Corinthians 1:3

I'VE ALWAYS ENCOURAGED my students and other believers not to feel like they have to fix everything when they have a friend who's hurting. When someone we care about is struggling through a trial, the temptation is to scramble to come up with all the answers. At other times, we may run from people because we don't know what to do or what to say—so we avoid a friend that really needs us. Neither of these approaches is best. We should care enough about

> **God gave us the Church for a reason—because he knew we were going to need each other.**

our loved ones and friends just to be there for them. Hug them. Put an arm around them. Listen to them. Pray with them.

But I learned that if you're the one who's hurting, you can't run away either. God gave us the Church for a reason—because he knew we were going to need each other. So people are going to say goofy stuff, and they're going to try to fix it, but the heart they demonstrate in all of that is what we need.

During my cancer ordeal, some of my loved ones and friends who knew me best really didn't offer much to say. But I could tell their hearts were all there for me. It mostly came in a hug that said, "We're with you." There wasn't a new truth for me to learn. It really was just walking in the truth I already knew. My closest friends confirmed for me that the right kind of silence can be golden in these tough seasons.

Most of the time, your hurting friends don't need a new sermon. They just need to know you're with them and you love them. Sit with them. Cry with them. Just be there.

Romans 12:15 says, "Rejoice with those who rejoice, weep with those who weep." That may be the most practical prescription ever. As you pray today, let your heart praise God for the people in your life who are rejoicing, and ask God for his comfort and blessings on those who weep. And then make sure you tell them how much you care. That's just another example of the very next thing you can do in his name.

Next Steps

✝ Where do I see myself in this?

✝ What is the next step God is showing me?

✝ My prayer:

Loving My Jesus

SUNDAY PRELUDE

ONE OF THE added blessings of being in Casting Crowns is that we get to be involved with a ministry called Teen Challenge. The word *teen* is in their name, but they help people of all ages who struggle with addictions or life-controlling problems.

If one of their centers is close to our venue, Teen Challenge brings their students to our concerts to serve as a part of our crew. I always know I'm going to have several touches with each student, so I try to get to know them throughout the day. I learn their names in the morning, ask them about something in their lives in the afternoon, then hopefully get a chance to deal with something they're going through before we pack up and leave.

At one particular stop, I met a guy I'll call Steve. He was probably 22 years old—a big, tall guy who wore a dark, heavy metal T-shirt, a denim vest, a long, curly beard, and hair to his shoulders. As big and mean as he wanted to look, I could tell he was hurting. I knew he had a soft heart just from talking to him during the morning. Life had beaten him down, and he didn't make much eye contact.

Later in the day, I invited Steve to come to the band's prayer time after sound check. When I started our devotional at prayer time, I turned to Psalm 63:1-4:

> *O God, you are my God; earnestly I seek you; my soul thirsts for you; my flesh faints for you, as in a dry and weary land where there is no water. So I have looked upon you in the sanctuary, beholding your power and glory. Because your steadfast love is better than life, my lips will praise you. So I will bless you as long as I live; in your name I will lift up my hands.*

I asked the group two questions: Have you figured out yet that you live in a dry and weary land? Are you looking for fulfillment and still think somewhere in the back of your mind that something in this world is going to do it for you?

"A lot of people are searching for something to fulfill them," I said. "We all want to get to the verse that says we want to see God in the sanctuary, behold his power and glory, and experience a love that is better than life. We want to skip to that verse, but we can't because we haven't resigned ourselves to the truth that this world cannot fill us. We first have to admit we're in a dry and weary land with no resources or rights of our own."

Steve heard the devotional and hung around afterward. I didn't get into anything deeply spiritual with him because he seemed a little aloof. He sat to the left of our soundboard and near our tech guys during the concert. I kept looking at him, because whenever I make a connection with one of the Teen Challenge guys—or anyone else I meet before our concerts— whatever I say onstage that night is for them. I often look straight at them. It focuses me better.

Steve appeared to be glued to everything he heard. He was a crew guy, so he was loving the lights and the music, but I sensed God working on his heart. After the show, I approached the crew and thanked all of the Teen Challenge guys and local volunteers for all of their work. I walked up to Steve and tried to see if I could break through his barrier.

"What do you think about everything you've heard?" I asked.

"Oh, I think it's real good. Real good."

I could tell that Jesus was redefining himself to Steve. Before that day, Steve did not have the correct picture of God. In Steve's head, God had picked others around him, because everything about his life said what he thought of himself: "I'm a crew guy. I'm the next class down. I'll never be in that group. I could never be one of the churchy people. I'll never be one of the people in front of everybody. This is just who I am in life."

I asked him how I could pray for him. He had a relative who was sick. I prayed for the relative and asked God to continue to pursue Steve and to stay in his thoughts and not let him take his mind off of anything he had heard that day.

Several weeks later, Steve showed up again at one of our concerts. He drove four hours to get there and brought his dad. He made a great connection with our drummer, Brian Scoggin. So the next day, when we were four more hours away, Steve showed up yet again and spent the day with Brian.

To my knowledge, Steve still hasn't repented and surrendered to Jesus.

Perhaps you figured that's where this story was headed—that Steve got saved and now he's serving in ministry somewhere. But I intentionally told Steve's story for this week's devotionals on the theme of "Loving My Jesus" because it's not a trophy account. See, the point isn't that we get another notch in our belts. The point is to be faithful to Jesus to do the very next thing he says.

God saves whom he wants to save, heals whom he wants to heal, and changes whom he wants to change. He doesn't hold me accountable for those areas. But he does desire me to be faithful to respond to his leading. He desires for me to go through every single day loving my Jesus, showing my scars, and telling my story of how mercy can reach them right where they are.

Key Passages of the Week: MATTHEW 28:16-20; ROMANS 10:9-13

YOUR STORY

"All authority in heaven and on earth has been given to me."
MATTHEW 28:18

FOR ABOUT FOUR years now, I've been working with the teenagers in my student ministry to teach them how to tell the story of their salvation. Every believer should be able to turn to a friend and say, "This is what God has done in my life." Who were you before you met Jesus? What happened when you met Jesus? What has happened since you started following Jesus? If you can answer those questions, you know your story. Every believer has a story whether they know how to articulate it yet or not.

A lot of believers are just like I was as a young man. We think our story is not compelling enough to make a difference in somebody's life. The Bible is full of people who walk on water or slay giants or split oceans, and all I did was grow up in church. I started going to church at eight years old and got saved when I was nine. I went to church pretty much every Sunday, but it wasn't until I was a young adult that I realized Jesus didn't have all of me. So I surrendered to him for ministry. On the surface, my story doesn't seem monumental enough to help anybody.

I've learned a few truths, however. One is that you never know how your story will resonate with someone. God may use one little nugget of an otherwise mundane life to prick someone's heart or make a meaningful connection. Your story may be a seed that blossoms in someone's life years later, and you may never even know it. Just be yourself, be faithful to share what God has done in your life, don't exaggerate, and be humble.

Your story may be a seed that blossoms in someone's life years later, and you may never know it.

Second, I've learned that people may try to dispute Scripture and even deny the deity of Christ. They may dismiss Christianity as a fairy tale. But one thing most people will never try to do is dispute your story. People will listen when you tell them that you were headed one direction, God changed you, and here's the result. They cannot deny that.

Finally, I've learned that it really doesn't matter what each of us thinks about our own story. In Matthew 28:19-20, Jesus' last instruction to his disciples before he ascended to heaven after his resurrection was, basically, "Go tell your story. Tell the world who I am. Tell them how I changed you. Tell them I can do the same for them." If we want to do the very next thing Jesus says now, a good place to start is the very last thing he said then.

NEXT STEPS

✝ Where do I see myself in this?

✝ What is the next step God is showing me?

✝ My prayer:

The Deepest Love

For the word of the cross is folly to those who are perishing, but to us who are being saved it is the power of God.

1 Corinthians 1:18

When Casting Crowns made its first record and began touring, we started performing at large festivals. Suddenly I went from being onstage in my church's gym on Wednesday nights to singing at events with artists like Toby Mac. I had one thought: "What am I doing on the same stage? He's got dancers and trampolines, and I'm a middle-aged student pastor with a Stars Wars T-shirt and nothing else up here. I'm not cool. I wasn't cool when I was young enough to be cool, and now I'm up here in front of 20,000 people."

Even today it gets to me when I have to sing alongside other artists who are better in pretty much every way. It's usually not until the middle of the first song that I remember, "Oh yeah, I'm just supposed to be myself here. I'm supposed to do what I do." And this is what I do: I generally stick to loving my Jesus, showing my scars, and telling my story.

Loving my Jesus comes first. We love on Jesus anytime we make much of him—anytime we decrease so he will increase. (John 3:30)

The deepest form of love is to sacrifice for someone, to spend time with someone. This is why loving on Jesus means digging deep into God's Word every day to get to know him more, letting God tell me who he is, who I was before I knew him, and who I am now that I'm in him. I constantly need to be reminded of my permanent, fixed identity. It seems that I'm always taking my eyes off of Jesus and looking down at the waves around me or comparing myself to people around me. I need to be reminded to stop sizing up people and thinking I'm the slow one in the room and that I'm the weak link—even questioning how God could possibly ever use me in this situation. Questioning how God could use me is putting too much stock in *me* instead of remembering that God is powerful enough to do anything he wants through anyone he wants. His power is not contingent on my gifts, and it's not at risk because of my shortcomings.

The more I'm in the Word, the more God shows me he uses the weak and "foolish" things to bring glory to himself. He filled the Bible full of people who had no other choice but to depend on him (Those accounts are their stories, by the way. Everyone has a story).

When I get out of the Word, it's identical to Peter taking his eyes off of Jesus as he walked on water. (Matthew 14:22-33) The moment I'm out of the Word, my eyes are on my situation instead of on him. So I really have to guard that time with him. I have to remember to keep on loving my Jesus.

NEXT STEPS

✝ Where do I see myself in this?

✝ What is the next step God is showing me?

✝ My prayer:

NO EXCUSES

The grace of our Lord overflowed for me with the faith
and love that are in Christ Jesus.

1 TIMOTHY 1:14

OUR SCARS ARE a huge part of our story. If we're not willing to let people see our scars, then we're not willing to let them see Jesus.

There's a danger anytime we say things like, "Yeah, I made that mistake, but everything happens for a reason." Well, the reason was probably because we were being idiots.

God doesn't want us to sin so we'll have a story. But we can trust that through suffering, when we go through the inevitable fallout of bad choices or apathy toward him, God still patiently steers us toward himself.

When people see you go through a hard time and come out walking with the Lord, those kinds of scars point to Jesus. Yes, self-inflicted scars that come from our choices can be embarrassing. We might be a little more ashamed to talk about them, but the world needs to hear about those kinds of scars. They need to hear, "Look, this is what happened when I chose that road, and this is where it took me."

In 1 Timothy 1:12-15, Paul knows he's done some stupid

stuff and makes no excuses for it. We all have creative ways to make excuses. We shouldn't excuse sin just because we sinned. We did something stupid. We should own that it was stupid. The reason we did it was because we were stupid. Stupid happens. Bad choices happen. We should accept the fact that if Paul was the chief of sinners then we have to be at least a lieutenant. I've done some of the dumbest things you could ever imagine, and they still affect me. The scars are still here.

We're all examples of what God can do, and he wants us on display.

But Paul makes sure he leaves us with hope and reminds us why we are to keep loving on Jesus. He says in the next verse, "I received mercy for this reason, that in me, the foremost of sinners, Jesus may *display* his perfect patience as an example."

We're all examples of what God can do, and he wants us on display. He wants us to show our scars because he knows their powerful impact.

Next Steps

✝ Where do I see myself in this?

✝ What is the next step God is showing me?

✝ My prayer:

AN EXAMPLE OF WHAT GOD CAN DO

Let those of us who are mature think this way.

PHILIPPIANS 3:15

TELLING YOUR STORY means learning how to share it in a purposed way that points to Jesus. It's a simple offering of what God has done in you as an example of what God can do in the person you're trying to reach.

God always arranges little moments for us to tell our stories. It's easy to wiggle out of these moments by rationalizing: "I feel like I have to be perfect before I share my faith. Well, I'm not perfect, and my friend knows almost everything I do. She knows when I get mad and kick the door. She knows what I say when someone gets on my nerves. She knows too much about me. I can't talk to her about Jesus."

But we're not talking about you saving her, are we? We're talking about Jesus saving her. If anything, the fact that you're saved even with your flaws ought to give her plenty of hope. You, as her friend, just have to be God's, warts and all. Sharing the love of Jesus *and* being transparent about your personal failures is probably one of the best witnesses you can offer.

I remember the first time I heard someone in ministry be transparent. I was a brand new youth pastor and attended a state evangelism conference to hear Dave Edwards speak. My world exploded. He talked about his dyslexia in front of a huge crowd after I'd spent years mastering how to hide the same condition. All I could think was, "What are you doing? You can't tell all of these people that you're dyslexic. They're going to think you're stupid. No one is going to listen to you now."

It was the first time I'd ever seen anybody be totally transparent and confess weakness in front of others, and I thought it was insane. Here I was making sure no one knew about my own dyslexia—calling on other people to read, or practicing my verse 10 times so I'd memorize it and not look dumb in Sunday School. And suddenly I see Dave Edwards being real. I remember Steven Curtis Chapman led worship in that same conference. He talked about his struggles and failings. The guy was a superstar, and he opened his heart to everyone. I thought, "Is this really all right to do? Can you really tell people that you don't have it all together?"

I felt a freedom I'd never experienced. I thought, "Man, I'm not the only one bumping my head on life here." I thank the Lord that I learned this truth early in my ministry. I realized I just need to be real. It's so much easier to listen to and share with somebody who's real, who has scars just like everyone else. In that sense, we should remember to use our scars as a road map to Jesus.

NEXT STEPS

✝ Where do I see myself in this?

✝ What is the next step God is showing me?

✝ My prayer:

The Benefits of Trials

That I may declare it boldly, as I ought to speak.

Ephesians 6:20

THE APOSTLE PAUL told the church in Philippi, "Hey, it's turned out to be a good thing that I'm here in prison, because it's evident to all the guards, to all the other prisoners, and to the brothers throughout the world that I'm here because of Jesus. I'm having an impact with my story" (paraphrased from Philippians 1:12-14).

Paul knew that how you handle a hard time speaks louder than your words. It speaks to people in authority over you. It speaks to people who don't know Jesus, because they see how you handle a storm. And even other Christians notice how you handle it. So Paul is in prison saying, "God has turned even what would appear to be horrible into something good for his glory. I'm going to be just fine." That's a special level of maturity.

One of the benefits of having cancer (yes, there are benefits to trials) is that suddenly you're a part of a large club full of members who understand your fear and pain. When new members join the club, you can love on them like no one else. I experienced this shortly after going through my own cancer surgery.

Scott Reeves is a faithful member of our church. I stopped by his business one day and he had surprising news. "I just got back from the doctor," he said. "I need you to pray for me. I have cancer." I listened to him for a few minutes as he sorted through his feelings, and I sensed a fellowship of suffering (Philippians 3:10).

All I said was, "I know how this moment feels. I've been here, and I know your world is rocked. So I'm praying for you." I didn't give him a dissertation or a sermon, because he knows all the Scripture. At the same time, that little piece of my story where I could identify with his pain helped build a bridge. So that's one way of telling your story—just letting someone know you're going to pray for him, or even praying for him right then on the spot. That's what I did with Scott. As we leaned against my truck, I prayed for him because he was about to tell his kids the news, and I know that feeling.

Telling your story and sharing your scars is your ministry. You're not a part of the audience of Christ; you're a part of the body of Christ, and this is what we do. We love Jesus. We show our scars. We tell our story. Every believer can do that. When we do, we are certain to be doing the very next thing God wants.

Some people in your world are never going to listen to a preacher, and they may never go to a church. But at some point you're going to find yourself sitting across from them at a café or working next to them in a cubicle. You have every-thing you need to point them to the Jesus you love.

NEXT STEPS

✝ Where do I see myself in this?

✝ What is the next step God is showing me?

✝ My prayer:

FAITHFUL TO WORK

For "everyone who calls on the name of the Lord will be saved."
ROMANS 10:13

SOMETHING HAPPENS INSIDE us when we share our faith. We may not be able to understand it, but we can sense it.

It's called spiritual growth. Paul described it in Philemon 1:6: "I pray that the sharing of your faith may become effective for the full knowledge of every good thing that is in us for the sake of Christ." That's a cool way of saying we'll never discover entire parts of our walk with Jesus until we start sharing our faith.

I used to have a hard time praying. My mind wandered in a million different directions. Then somebody told me, "Just pray out loud," and it worked. I learned that when I put my concerns into spoken words, my brain doesn't roam all over the place. It has to decide to do something, and my prayer becomes more focused.

It's the same with sharing our faith. We may understand the concept of the truth and accept the truth and even live by the truth. But until we have to form sentences to articulate what we believe, the concept remains mostly just that: a concept. It doesn't mean we're any less saved, but God somehow takes our relationship with him to a deeper personal level when we are willing to go public with our faith in him. I believe this is why Romans 10:9 says we are to confess with our mouths what our hearts believe.

We don't really own what we believe until we can give it to somebody. When someone tries to explain a concept to you, you may hear it and take it in, but until you can explain it to someone else, you don't understand it as well as you may think.

Ask any young believer what it takes to be saved. You'll get about a five-minute answer. She will start and re-start and then realize something she forgot, and she's not sure what to include because she hasn't said it before.

But when we work out our salvation by working on how to tell people about Jesus, we narrow our story to a powerful focus. At first, we may stumble a bit with our words. That's OK. Once you do the very next thing Jesus says to do, sharing your story and your scars, confidence follows.

Some people will reject truth and reject Jesus. But truth spoken in love stays after you leave. Your friend may decline to respond to what you say on the spot, but your words will stay on her mind if for no other reason than you cared enough to share with her. When you're faithful to share the gospel, Jesus is faithful to work. You will see him save others. You also will grow in confidence toward your Savior as you see him totally change people, like he changed you, when it seemed they were beyond hope.

NEXT STEPS

✝ Where do I see myself in this?

✝ What is the next step God is showing me?

✝ My prayer:

Make Me a River

SUNDAY PRELUDE

Jesus pitied the sight.

As if he could be contained in a golden pitcher. As if the pitcher had to be made of gold. As if the water in the pitcher had to come from a certain place. As if all the pomp made the moment holy. As if another ceremony brought those solemn priests any closer to the God they professed.

As if profession without confession, without repentance, is worth the time they spent lighting lamps and carrying water.

It was the seventh and final day of the Feast of Tabernacles, the most popular of Israel's three major religious feasts. The Jews celebrated the fall harvest of grapes and olives with this feast each year, ascending to Jerusalem from throughout Palestine to erect tiny booths, or tabernacles, in remembrance of their ancestors' forty years in the wilderness. Lately, Jesus had stirred the masses by teaching in the temple and confounding and angering the Jewish religious elite. They were the ones who lit all the lamps and carried the ceremonial pitcher of water to symbolize the very Messiah with whom they had argued just days before.

Imagine how Jesus felt. Imagine the creator and God of the universe as he looked with a mix of compassion and frustration at the people who had come to worship him and didn't know it—the same people who had come to berate him yet knew not what they did.

And now, just as they had done the previous six days of the feast, here came the three priests again, right on schedule. They made their way to the Water Gate as the High Priest held the golden pitcher filled with water from the Pool of Siloam. Three short trumpet blasts preceded the people's recitation of Isaiah 12:3:

> *"With joy you will draw water from the wells of salvation. And you will say in that day: 'Give thanks to the Lord, call upon his name, make known his deeds among the peoples, proclaim that his name is exalted.'"*

Jesus watched it all, longing for them to exalt his name.

Once the procession reached the temple, the priests marched the water pitcher around the altar as the temple choir sang the Hallel, or Psalm 113-118.

Off to the side, Jesus listened as the choir in only their sixth verse sang of the Lord "who humbles Himself to behold the things that are in the heavens and in the earth" (Psalm 113:6 NKJV).

That very Lord who had humbled himself to behold the proceedings had seen enough. Indignant at all the dignity, all the empty ritual, Jesus stood and cried out.

"If anyone thirsts, let him come to me and drink. Whoever believes in me, as the Scripture has said, 'Out of his heart will flow rivers of living water'" (John 7:37-38).

And with that came a hush as Jesus turned more lofty heads.

Key Passages of the Week: ROMANS 5:1-5; COLOSSIANS 3:1-17; JAMES 2:14-26

LIVE FOR THE OUTLETS

Through him we have also obtained access by faith into this grace in which we stand.
ROMANS 5:2

SEVERAL YEARS AGO, I visited Israel and traveled to both the Sea of Galilee and the Dead Sea. Both are large bodies of water fed by fresh water. The Sea of Galilee in the northern part of the country is vibrant and full of life and for centuries has provided a living for fishermen like the disciples Peter, James, and John. The Dead Sea, positioned to the east and southeast of Jerusalem, has its name for a reason. It is so salty that not much can live in it and a human being can float with little effort.

> **We should pray for God to make us a river, for his living water to flow through us and impact others for his glory.**

The freshwater Jordan River flows south from the Sea of Galilee and straight into the Dead Sea. So why is the Sea of Galilee so vibrant and the Dead Sea so dead? Why is it roughly nine times saltier than Earth's oceans? Because the Sea of Galilee has outlets whereas the Dead Sea has none. Water flows into the Dead Sea, but nothing flows out. The water settles into a lake that, at 1,407 feet below sea level, is the planet's lowest elevation point on land.

We should pray for God to make us a river, for his living water to flow through us and impact others for his glory. Jesus alone is the source of our strength and hope, and Romans 5:5 gives us the incredible promise that "hope does not put us to shame, because God's love has been poured into our hearts through the Holy Spirit who has been given to us."

This same Holy Spirit is the living water that flows through us, spilling out God's love as it overflows from his heart through our hearts and into others' lives. One verse after Jesus claims to be the source of eternal living water, John explains what he meant: "Now this he said about the Spirit, whom those who believed in him were to receive" (John 7:39).

The point of doing the very next thing for Jesus is not to dream up ideas on our own. Rather, we are to stay intimately connected to the Lord by spending time in Scripture, prayer, and worship, and to live with an eternal perspective. That means keeping our hearts and minds on things above, where our destination is, and not on earthly, fleshly pursuits. Then we will see where Jesus is at work and where people are low and hurting as surely as water finds its way to the lowest point.

NEXT STEPS

✝ Where do I see myself in this?

✝ What is the next step God is showing me?

✝ My prayer:

COLOSSIANS 3:1-17

———

TURNING INWARD

Set your minds on things that are above, not on things that are on earth.
COLOSSIANS 3:2

ONE OF THE surest ways to become your own Dead Sea is to refuse to be a conduit through which Jesus' living water can flow. The Christian who has become stagnant and stale almost certainly has ceased seeking out ways to pour into others.

You're not a pond. You're a river. Everything that God pours into you is for you to pour into somebody else.

Living water not only has tributaries (streams and rivers that "pay tribute" to it by feeding it); it also has a place to go to continue living. In the same way, nothing we try to do in our own motives ever satisfies or has any lasting effect. Something dies when we turn inward and the object of our focus becomes ourselves.

I struggled with this one when Casting Crowns' first album started gaining traction. Early on, I watched the charts to see how our songs were doing. Our management and label in Nashville sent email updates like, "Hey, we did such-and-such in record sales this week, and the song is number one."

I found myself checking my email an awful lot and looking for phone calls from area code 615 in Nashville,

Tennessee. I wanted to hear the latest awesome news and discover what record we had broken.

When the Lord convicted me, a cold dose of reality dawned on me.

"You know, this isn't always going to happen," I said. "We're popular right now, but what happens when the song doesn't go number one? What happens when the record does- n't sell as much as the previous one?"

I realized I had turned inward. I felt the emptiness of rankings and headlines. I wanted to feel alive again, so I asked the Lord to guide my every step and to protect me from myself and keep me from wandering away. I called our manager and other people in Nashville.

"I don't need to know how things are going," I said. "Just don't let me know. Whatever happens, happens."

Now I hear things through the grapevine after the fact. We've had records go platinum and it surprised me when I eventually heard it. Our song would be number one, and the band wouldn't even know it. We decided to build the ministry on Jesus and his Word rather than Billboard and its charts.

It's fine if an area of your life motivates and inspires you, but it's not okay if it becomes your reason for living. It's fine to draw satisfaction from your successes, but it's crippling if you draw your identity from them. What you do, even the things you do for Jesus, is not who you are. Who you are in Christ—forgiven, redeemed, a saint, a child of God, a co-heir with Christ—is your real identity.

NEXT STEPS

✝ Where do I see myself in this?

✝ What is the next step God is showing me?

✝ My prayer:

FRANK THOUGHTS

So whoever knows the right thing to do and fails to do it, for him it is a sin.
JAMES 4:17

GOD MAKES PREPARATIONS for his saints. He is with you and will equip you for his plans. He will help himself to your life and make you a river if you are willing.

Dr. Adrian Rogers once preached a series on the book of Genesis in which he gave an interesting math lesson from Genesis 5:25-29:

> *"When Methuselah had lived 187 years, he fathered Lamech. Methuselah lived after he fathered Lamech 782 years and had other sons and daughters. Thus all the days of Methuselah were 969 years, and he died. When Lamech had lived 182 years, he fathered a son and called his name Noah."*

In Genesis 7:6, we learn that Noah was 600 years old when God sent the Great Flood to destroy mankind in its wickedness. Don't get caught up wondering why men lived so long back then in that radically different pre-Flood world— the point to follow is the math. It shows us that Methuselah lived exactly 600 years after Noah was born. That's when the

Flood came. Do you know why God had Enoch give his baby the name *Methuselah*? Because in Hebrew the name means, "It shall be sent when he is dead."

Methuselah lived 969 years as evidence of the mercy of a longsuffering God who promised righteous judgment but gave people time to repent. The Flood was sent when he died. But God in his patience waited and waited, and that's why Methuselah lived longer than any other human being in history.

If God can renew the world through a Flood announced by a baby nearly 1,000 years earlier, that means he possibly, might, *just maybe* have a specific idea of what he wants you to do next.

Sometimes Jesus is frank with us. He tells us to go fix our relationships before we even try to worship him (Matthew 5:23-25). He tells us we can't be his disciples if we don't die to ourselves, pick up our cross, and follow him. He tells us we have to lose our lives for his sake (Matthew 24:26). He tells us that our love for him must be so strong that our love for our family seems like hate in comparison (Luke 14:26).

If God worked patiently for 969 years to unfold his plan in the days of Noah, surely he is still at work now that, as Jesus said, the kingdom of God has come.

So here's another frank thought for you: What are you certain Jesus wants you to do today? Are you willing to do it now? Maybe it was the very next thing at one point, and you've been putting it off for months, maybe even years. If you know Jesus still would have you do it, are you willing to do it right now, today?

Are you?

Next Steps

✝ Where do I see myself in this?

✝ What is the next step God is showing me?

✝ My prayer:

EPHESIANS 6:10-12

BEND IN THE RIVER

For we do not wrestle against flesh and blood, but against the rulers, against the authorities, against the cosmic powers over this present darkness, against the spiritual forces of evil in the heavenly places.

EPHESIANS 6:12

AS WE AVAIL ourselves to be God's river in others' lives, we will hit rocky stretches. Almost always, those rocks will be people—even the ones we're trying to help.

Paul says our struggle is not against flesh and blood but against the powers of darkness that have fooled people into the lives they're living. So people are not the enemy. I can't tell you how many times I've heard, "I'm trying to live for God, but my boss is unfair and he's holding me down." Or I've heard, "I'm trying to live for Jesus at school, but this atheist teacher is riding me, and I'm just going to stand up and let him have it."

You may be right. Someone may be making your life difficult. But instead of trying to create a big, bad wolf, we should remember that people are never the enemy.

The enemy is the devil, who is fooling your boss or teacher or spouse into the life he or she is leading. God loves those people just as much as he loves you. Those folks have a hole inside that only Jesus can fill, but sin is clouding their view. Now they're just begging on the inside for someone to prove them wrong.

There aren't good people and bad people. Instead, there are people who know Jesus and people who need to know Jesus. It's hard to see people that way when they're close to you or even hurting you. Maybe your boss won't let you off on Sundays, or your teacher won't listen to you and makes fun of you in class because you're a Christian. Maybe your friend on the wrong road is self-absorbed, dominates the conversation, and won't listen to anything you say.

Remember that people are just people. They're lost, but they're sincere, they want to succeed, and they want to be happy and loved. They don't want to destroy themselves; they're just going off of their guts. Paul says their god is their stomach and their glory is their shame (Philippians 3:19). If that's the case, how do you think people whose god is their gut are going to act? They're going to respond by going after what feeds them at the moment, what scratches their itches and seems most likely to satisfy their ever-empty stomach.

By allowing living water to flow through you, you provide your desperate friends the only true fountain of life. You may be the only source of this living water in their lives. So pray for Jesus to make you a river, and then allow him to bend you wherever he wants you to flow.

Next Steps

✝ Where do I see myself in this?

✝ What is the next step God is showing me?

✝ My prayer:

PROOF

Show me your faith apart from your works, and I will show you my faith by my works.
JAMES 2:18

SOMETIMES WHEN WE'RE at church it seems as if everything is abstract and grandiose. We hear an epic Bible verse that sounds reserved for Super Christians. We listen to a missionary's testimony of a sold-out life that scares us. We sing a lyric in a song that sounds meaningful but doesn't connect to our real lives. These are not steps we can actually take—or things we can actually do—and it seems the issue is even grayer now that we're scared to death of works in our grace culture. We're petrified to say that, as a believer, you might actually need to do something.

As we come full circle in our study, let's remember that God saw fit to make the book of Acts the very next thing he showed us after giving us the Gospels. The book of Acts literally is a book of actions. Chronologically, the Gospel happened, and then all of Acts happened. The book of Acts is a testimony of how the people whom God had saved and redeemed became that spring of living water that he revealed to the woman at the well. It was just a concept before. Then it became actions.

And somehow they got it. But often we don't get it. We're

not really sure how everything is supposed to unfold.

Sometimes we are frozen by our own guilt over sin. Sometimes feelings of unworthiness limit us. At the other end of the spectrum, sometimes we can be so judgmental of others that we don't want to lift a finger.

I'm with the Apostle James, who said faith without works is dead. He preached not that works save us, but that they are proof we are saved:

"So also faith by itself, if it does not have works, is dead. But someone will say, 'You have faith and I have works.' Show me your faith apart from your works, and I will show you my faith by my works." *(James 2:17-18)*

Paul says we're saved by faith (Romans 3:28; 5:1). And then James says, "Your works are what prove you even have faith." The answer is faith works. That's it. True faith goes and works. Works that aren't motivated by faith are dead, and faith that doesn't get up and work is not real.

While it may sound like Paul is saying one thing and James is saying another, they're actually complementary. In 1 Thessalonians 1:3, Paul combines the two and refers to our "work of faith and labor of love." We have a working faith. Paul is saying our labor comes from our love, and our works come from our faith.

Over the long haul, if the very next things you do remain constant, God-honoring, and selfless, they will display that your faith is real.

NEXT STEPS

✝ Where do I see myself in this?

✝ What is the next step God is showing me?

✝ My prayer:

Saturday

PHILIPPIANS 3:7-11

PERFECT LOVE

That I may know him and the power of his resurrection.

PHILIPPIANS 3:10

GUARD AGAINST THE trap of thinking the very next thing is a checklist. That approach is a Pharisee's lie in which, instead of knowing God intimately, all I know are the dos and don'ts and the rules and routines. And I also know this: I feel terrible.

So what do I do? I resort back to the cycle, and before long I'm thinking, "I've got to do better. I've got to try harder. I've got to sing louder. I've got to read more. What was I doing back when my life was going great? The stuff. I've got to do the stuff better."

> **Our obedience should be an unbridled response to what God has done in our lives.**

So now I'm traipsing around in a giant circle. Why? Because I'm attempting to earn a love that was never meant to be earned. It was a gift.

The answer is in Revelation 2:4, when Jesus says, in effect, "Listen, you're doing all the stuff. But you've forgotten your first love. You were so in love with me. What happened?"

Our obedience should be an unbridled response to what God has done in our lives. When that becomes our mission, we're truly worshipping God with our lives. That's the hope to which he has called us. The cool thing about God living in us is we are never, ever, ever going to be alone again. Ever.

It doesn't matter if you're in a room full of people or in the solitude of a quiet house and broken home. It doesn't matter how the emptiness feels or what degree the temptation. It doesn't matter what the boss, friend, or relative says. You are never by yourself.

Since Christ is with us all the way, he will funnel his living water through us as we abide in him and deluge ourselves in his Word and in a walk of obedience to his commands (John 15:1-17). And 1 John 2:3-5 says that when our actions prove that we are in love with Jesus, they become the very mechanism he uses to assure us he is with us.

> *And by this we know that we have come to know him, if we keep his commandments. Whoever says 'I know him' but does not keep his commandments is a liar, and the truth is not in him, but whoever keeps his word, in him truly the love of God is perfected.*

The love of God is perfected when we keep his Word and do the very next thing for his glory.

NEXT STEPS

✝ Where do I see myself in this?

✝ What is the next step God is showing me?

✝ My prayer:

Phase One:

Since the book of Acts is a book of actions, since it is the record of the disciples and the early Church acting on the gospel they'd just been given, it's a great book to study. For the next four weeks, read one chapter of Acts per day. You'll be finished in 28 days. After each chapter, ask yourself the following #OperationNEXT questions about each chapter:

- What is God saying about himself?
- What is God saying about me?
- Do I find myself in any of the people?
- Is there a promise I need to claim?
- Is there part of me I need to lay down?
- Who am I going to share this with? (Remember you're not a pond, you're a river. Everything you read is not just for you.)
- What is my next step?

Phase Two:

Let's start a revolution. A lost and dying world is starving for the simplicity of Christ's love. I ask you the favor of participating in an experiment. You've spent six weeks immersed in the truths of Scripture about following God by doing the very next thing he asks you to do. You know his Word. You've sensed his Spirit. Now prove you're sincere.

Week Seven of this study is a worldwide lab. For the next seven days, pray each day for God to show you the very next thing he wants you to do in his name that day. When he leads you to it, act on it. Then post a thumbnail description of what happened on social media and close the post with #OperationNEXT. Put it on Twitter, Facebook, Instagram, another preferred media, or all of the above.

If someone asks you what #OperationNEXT means, use it as a great segue to tell your story, show your scars, and love on Jesus. Abandonment isn't so scary when we're all in it together. Let's follow Jesus into the very next thing and see what happens.

———

For more individual copies or bulk orders of *The Very Next Thing*, please visit www.castingcrowns.com.

———

Also from Mark Hall with Tim Luke:

Lifestories
Your Own Jesus
The Well
Thrive